Route Finding
Navigating with Map and Compass

Gregory Crouch

FALCON®

HELENA, MONTANA

A **FALCON** GUIDE®

Falcon® is continually expanding its list of recreational guidebooks. All books include detailed descriptions, accurate maps, and all the information necessary for enjoyable trips. You can order extra copies of this book and get information and prices for other Falcon® guidebooks by writing Falcon, P.O. Box 1718, Helena, MT 59624 or calling toll-free 1-800-582-2665. Please ask for a free copy of our current catalog. Visit our website at www.FalconOutdoors.com or contact us by e-mail at falcon@falcon.com.

© 1999 Falcon® Publishing, Inc., Helena, Montana
Printed in Canada.

2 3 4 5 6 7 8 9 0 TP 04 03 02 01 00

Library of Congress Cataloging-in-Publication Data

Crouch, Gregory, 1966–
    Route finding : navigating with map and compass / Gregory
Crouch.
        p. cm.
    ISBN 1-56044-820-2 (pbk.)
    1. Orienteering. 2. Navigation. 3. Map reading. 4. Compass.
I. Title.
GV200.4.C76   1999
796.58—dc21   99-25394
                                                           CIP

CAUTION

Outdoor recreation can be dangerous, including hiking and backpacking. Everyone who goes into the wilderness or backcountry assumes some risk and responsibility for his or her own actions and safety.

The information contained in this book is a summary of the author's personal experiences, research, review of existing literature on backpacking, guiding experience, and conversations with backpacking experts. However, neither this book (nor any other book) can assure your safety from the elements. Nor can this book (or any other book) replace sound judgment and good decision-making skills, which will greatly reduce the risks of going into the wilderness.

Learn as much as possible from this book and other sources of information, and prepare for the unexpected. Be cautious. The reward will be a safer and more enjoyable experience.

To my parents, Janet Crouch and Robert Crouch, for giving me legs and the will to use them

Contents

Introduction

To read a map, you need to understand the language of maps—a pictorial language that communicates with lines, colors, and symbols. As you come to love and understand maps and wilderness route finding, you'll come to appreciate how the central problem of land navigation mirrors one of life's great problems: One of the hardest things to know is where you stand *Right Now*. It's easy to know where you're going—toward some distant goal—be it getting a degree, being chosen for a big promotion, starting a family, or buying a dream home—but it's not so easy to know where you are at any given moment. That's also the fundamental problem in land navigation.

In the wilderness, as in life, it is easy to know where you want to go—to that renowned lake, distant mountaintop, or spectacular campsite—but if you don't know where you are *Right Now*, you won't be able to figure out how to reach your objective. In fact, if you don't know where you are (i.e., if you can't mark that exact spot on the map), you're lost. And it's much easier to always know where you are than it is to get oriented once you've lost the way. This book will teach you how to read maps and determine your location at all times.

Once you know where you are *Right Now*, your map can give you vast amounts of information. It can tell you the name of that beautiful mountain at the head of the valley, how far it is to the next stream, or, if it's your last day on the trail, how far it is to the parking lot. Your map will allow you to show a rescue team *exactly* where you left that injured hiker when you went for help. Or, if you come to an unexpected, unsigned fork in the trail, your map will help you make an informed guess about which path to choose. But all of this works only if you know where you are *Right Now*.

Besides being of immense practical value while you're on the trail, a map can help you plan a trip before you ever leave home. You probably can't plan coherently without one. A map makes it possible to plan a journey across a great, unseen distance. If you're able to skillfully interpret its language, a map will tell you how far it is between campsites, how much water you're likely to encounter, how steep the trail is, and how much elevation you will gain; it will also help you decide what clothing and equipment to carry.

Like anything worth knowing, route finding and land navigation aren't always easy to learn. They're disciplines that take much effort to master. And you will make mistakes along the way, so learn from them. Go outside, practice, and enjoy. Learn how to navigate and you will become a safer, more competent outdoorsperson—it is a cornerstone skill.

Map Basics

A map is a simplified picture of the real world that uses colors, labels, and graphic symbols to represent features found on the surface of the earth. A map is a two-dimensional tool that helps us visualize and understand something inherently three-dimensional—the earth's surface—even parts of it we have not seen.

MAP TYPES

There are many different kinds of maps, because different maps serve different purposes. Here's a list of common map types: **Geographic maps** provide information about a mapped area with regard to climate, population distribution, relief, vegetation, or other such general geographic data. **Road maps** show main transportation networks, urban areas, and major points of interest. **Ridgeline maps** don't show much detail—they're just terrain drawings of an area's major features, such as peaks, ridges, streams, and rivers. These maps are used for navigation in exotic, far-off lands where wilderness areas are not carefully mapped. **Topographic maps** portray horizontal and vertical terrain with the use of colors, symbols, and contour lines (lines of constant elevation), which allow us to visualize the three-dimensional size and shape of the landscape.

Other common map types include city maps, field sketches, historical maps, and nautical charts. Topographic maps are far and away the most useful maps for the outdoor traveler. This book focuses on the use of topographic maps for wilderness navigation.

NAVIGATION EQUIPMENT

In addition to a map or maps of the area through which you intend to travel, there are a few other items of equipment you need to complete your navigator's kit:

- A good, durable compass. Unfortunately, a decent compass is expensive, but it's worth the investment to buy a good one. Cheap ones can't handle wilderness abuse.
- A mechanical pencil with a fine point (and plenty of lead). I recommend a mechanical pencil because, unlike a pen, it will not run when wet. When a previously ink-marked map gets wet, the ink runs all over the place. Remember too that it is almost impossible to write on a damp or wet map with either pencil or ink.
- A protractor for measuring angles. Square protractors are easiest to use, but other kinds will work. Just make sure to buy one that has at least one straight edge, so you won't need to carry a ruler.
- A zipper-locked bag.
- An altimeter (optional). Climbers like these devices, which can help fix your position when used with a topographic map.

Note: *For a detailed checklist of survival and first-aid items, see* Backpacking Tips *(Falcon 1998).*

Topographic Maps

Topographic maps are scale drawings of the earth's surface that use lines of constant elevation, called **contour lines,** to depict the ups and downs of the landscape. Contour lines make it possible to understand the three-dimensional size and shape of landforms printed on a two-dimensional surface. In addition to contour lines, topographic maps use a standard set of colors and symbols to represent other features.

SCALE

To be of much practical value, the picture drawn by a map must accurately represent the terrain the map attempts to portray. To accomplish this, maps are drawn to scale, which means that a certain distance on the map corresponds to a certain distance on the earth's surface. A map's scale, which resembles a fraction, is the ratio between map distance and real-world distance. So, on a map with a scale of 1:50,000, 1 inch on the map equals 50,000 inches on the ground. In conversation, map scales are often referred to as a "one-to-fifty," for a 1:50,000 map or a "one-to-twenty-four," for a map with a scale of 1:24,000.

Scale = Map Distance : Ground Distance

Maps come in three basic categories of scale: small, medium, and large. These categories are confusing, because a small-scale map shows a lot more land than a large-scale map. The larger the second number of the ratio, the smaller the scale. So a 1:1,000,000 map is a smaller scale than a 1:50,000 map because 1/1,000,000th of something is a lot smaller than 1/50,000th of the same thing.

The large-scale/small-scale quandary is easy to understand if you think in terms of detail instead of land area. A large-scale map shows a lot more detail than a small-scale one. Select a map based on what you intend to do with it.

Large Scale Map = More Detail = Small Area of Land

Small Scale Map = Less Detail = Large Area of Land

Small-scale maps, those with scales smaller than 1:1,000,000, are maps of big things—counties, states, provinces, countries, and continents—that don't show much specific geographic detail. You would use a small-scale map to plan a driving tour or a trip to a foreign land.

Medium-scale maps are maps with scales between 1:1,000,000 and 1:75,000. Medium-scale maps (quadrangles, for example) show a moderate amount of the earth's surface and a moderate amount of detail. They are useful for planning long backcountry excursions that will cover many miles. The most common medium-scale maps are 1:100,000 scale, usually referred to as "30- x 60-minute quads."

Large-scale maps have scales larger than 1:75,000. Large-scale maps show a lot of detail. You should have a large-scale map in hand when you are out in the wilderness finding your way. The most common large-scale maps include: 1:24,000 scale, referred to as a "7.5 minute quad," which is used for precise navigation; 1:50,000 scale, common in metric countries and used by the military; 1:62,500 scale, referred to as a "15 minute quad," which is used for general-purpose backcountry travel. This series has been discontinued by the U.S. Geological Survey, but you will still often see this scale on commercially produced maps for popular areas.

The term "minutes" refers to the standard system of longitude and latitude which uses 360 degrees, 60 minutes per degree, and 60 seconds per minute to locate any spot on earth. (See Chapter 10 for a more detailed explanation.) A 1-degree map covers 1 degree of longitude, while a 15-minute map covers one quarter of one degree of longitude.

We regularly use maps of each scale: a small-scale highway map to find the way to a trailhead by car, a medium-scale topographic map to make the overall plan for a backpacking trip, and several adjoining large-scale topographic maps with a lot of detail for day-to-day navigation in the backcountry.

Where do you find the scale of a map? In a map's margin—along with a lot of other useful information.

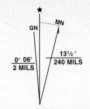

**UTM GRID AND 1972 MAGNETIC NORTH
DECLINATION AT CENTER OF SHEET**

Declination diagram

QUADRANGLE LOCATION

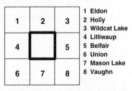

ADJOINING 7.5' QUADRANGLE NAMES

Quadrangle location and adjoining map sheets

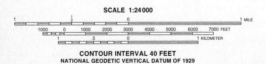

**CONTOUR INTERVAL 40 FEET
NATIONAL GEODETIC VERTICAL DATUM OF 1929**

Map scale, bar scales, and contour intervals

MARGINAL INFORMATION

The margin of a topographic map is full of symbols, draw-ings, and technical writing; and this stuff is called, not surprisingly, marginal information. Some of the marginal information is, well, marginal, but amid the technical jar-gon is a lot of important stuff. Learn to find the map's name, scale, bar scales, contour interval, declination diagram, and adjoining sheet names in a map's margin.

The following list indicates the important marginal in-formation on maps made by the U.S. Geological Survey and other agencies and companies.

- **Map name:** at the top and bottom right-hand corners.
- **The year the map was made:** with the fine print in the lower left-hand corner.
- **The scale:** in the upper center of the bottom margin.
- **Bar scales:** just below the map scale—long lines with distance information. Most maps have three bar scales: one to indicate distance in miles, another to indicate distance in feet, and a third for distance in meters and kilometers.
- **Contour interval:** below the bar scales—indicates what the vertical distance is between the lines of constant elevation.
- **Declination diagram:** to the left of the bar scales— shows the difference between true north, magnetic north, and grid north or map north.

- **Adjoining map sheets:** The names of the maps (in the same series) that adjoin each edge of your map are printed in each margin.
- **Legend:** in the margin—explains the various symbols used on the map.

COLOR

Maps print different types of geographic and cultural information in different colors. The topographic map colors usually have the following meaning:

Brown: Used for relief and elevation. Contour lines and elevation numbers are printed in brown (except on glaciers and permanent snowfields, where they are shown in blue).

Green: Areas of vegetation, such as forests or orchards.

White: Areas of little or no vegetation.

Blue: Water, including lakes, streams, rivers, swamps, and oceans. Contour lines on glaciers and permanent snowfields are also shown in blue.

Black: Names, boundaries, buildings, railroads, roads, trails, and manmade features.

Red: Important roads.

MAP SYMBOLS

The U.S. Geological Survey, makers of the most commonly used topographic maps, have established a standard set of symbols to represent features of the landscape. A complete list and key for all topographic symbols is available from the U.S. Geological Survey (see the appendix for contact information).

CONTOUR LINES

Topographic maps use imaginary lines of constant elevation, called contour lines, to represent three dimensions with two. All points on the same contour line are the same distance above or below sea level, and the vertical interval (called the contour interval) between the contour lines is the same everywhere on the map. Every fifth contour line is twice as thick as its neighbors (called **intermediate contours**). These bold brown lines are called **index contours** and are often printed with their elevations.

It's important to learn to visualize the three-dimensional features of the real world from the information provided by contour lines. The ability to visualize the size and shape of three-dimensional terrain from contour lines is the true "art" of map reading. A cone sitting on a flat table looks like this when depicted with contour lines:

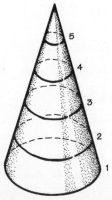

Cone   *Depicted with contour lines*

A hill in an otherwise featureless landscape might look like this:

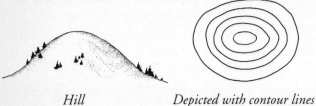

Hill   *Depicted with contour lines*

Contour lines show the **slope** as well as the **shape** of terrain. The closer the contour lines are together, the steeper the slope. Contour lines that are far apart show terrain that is flat or gently sloped.

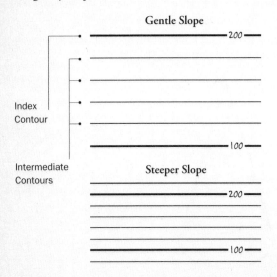

Slope gradient reflected in spacing of contour lines

To Calculate the Elevation of an Intermediate Contour Line

1. Find the index contour lines above and below the intermediate contour. Trace along them to find their elevation lines.

2. Find the map's contour interval (in the margin, below the bar scales).

3. From the nearest index contour, count up or down, adding or subtracting one increment of the contour interval for every contour line you cross until you get to the line whose elevation you want to know.

TERRAIN FEATURES

Fortunately, despite the convoluted appearance of topographic maps, there are only ten different types of basic terrain features. They are depicted visually on pages 18 and 19.

Spurs and ridges are essentially the same, just like valleys and draws are essentially the same. It's a question of size: Ridges are bigger than spurs, and valleys are bigger than draws. Draws and spurs are typically more rugged and steep-sided than their larger cousins.

The real world is a complex and convoluted place, and terrain features do not exist in isolation. Page 21 shows, on a large-scale topographic map, how the various pieces of the terrain puzzle can fit together to form a landscape.

Major Terrain Features

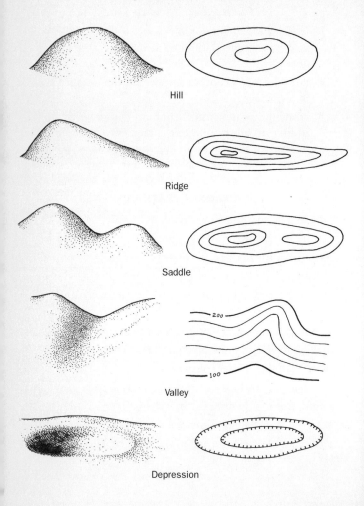

Hill

Ridge

Saddle

Valley

Depression

Minor Terrain Features

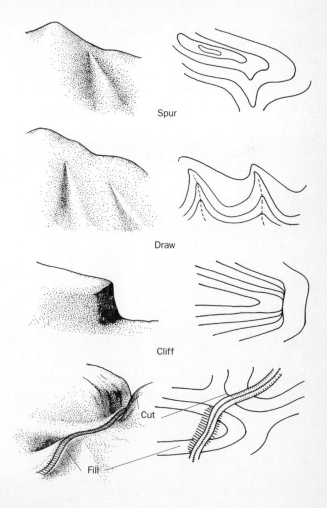

Spur

Draw

Cliff

Cut

Fill

Some Tips to Help You Visualize the Shape of the Landscape

Contour lines are perfectly flat. They don't go uphill or downhill, and they form closed loops. It is easy to confuse ridges with valleys, and draws with spurs, because the contour lines formed by all four features make V's and U's. When you're trying to sort out those twisting and turning contour lines, remember that:

- The blue lines that depict streams or rivers are found in valleys and draws, although streams are not found in *every* valley or draw.

- In valleys and draws contour lines make V's or U's—the point of the V or the curve of the U points uphill. Use two index contours to determine which way is up. V's indicate steep slopes, and U's indicate gentler slopes.

- The contour lines formed by ridges and spurs also make V's or U's—the point of the V or the curve of the U points downhill. Use two index contours to determine which way the terrain slopes.

- Streams merge in valleys or draws; the single leg of the blue Y, formed where two streams meet, almost always points downhill. (The exception is when a river or stream breaks into two or more channels around an island.)

- Depressions are relatively rare—small, concentric circles almost always indicate hills or mountaintops.

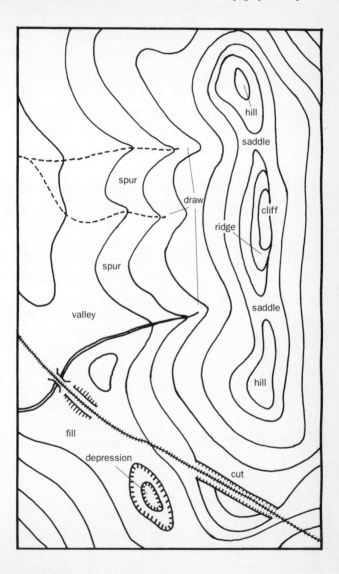

Why Every Undulation in the Landscape
Does Not Appear on the Map

It's a fact of mapmaking that small features in the landscape do not always appear on topographic maps. A 39-foot hill does not appear on a map with a 40-foot contour interval. Likewise, on the same map, you can be walking across a landscape that your map shows to be flat and featureless and stumble across an impassable 35-foot cliff.

However, despite the fact that a small hilltop on a rising ridge may not appear as a separate, identifiable feature on the map, the contour lines that do exist can offer clues about what has been omitted.

The larger the contour interval, the more detail is lost. For example, mountainous regions are often depicted with contour intervals of 100 or 200 feet (otherwise the maps

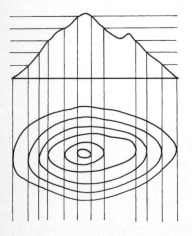

How small terrain features can "disappear." Note the missing hilltop and the "footprint" left on the otherwise constantly sloped ridge.

would be an indecipherable clutter of nearly merging brown lines). Significant hills, slopes, rock towers, and cliffs may not always appear on these maps.

⬡ NAVIGATION TIP

Contour lines don't tell you whether a steep slope is passable or not. A set of closely packed contours might be a steady slope that you could scramble up with ease, or a cliff that only a mountaineer could negotiate.

DISTANCE BETWEEN TWO POINTS

The fact that topographic maps are drawn to scale allows us to calculate the real-world distance between two points from the map distance between those two points. Scale relates map distance to ground distance, as explained earlier.

Distance measured on a map will always be short of real-world distance, because map distance does not account for the ups and downs of real terrain. Therefore, be aware that the distance your feet will have to travel will always be more than it appears on the map.

Measuring Straight-line Distance

1. Use the straight edge of a piece of scrap paper, a piece of string or dental floss, or a ruler to measure the map distance between two points.
2. Calculate the ground distance by laying the measured distance against one of the bar scales found in the bottom

margin. Careful! The zero is often *not* at the left edge of the bar scale, but a short distance inside the bar (see the illustration below).

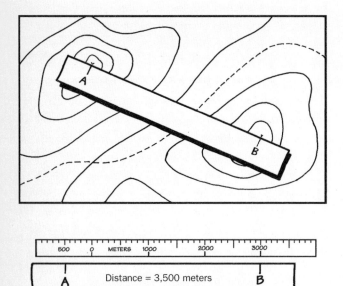

Measuring straight-line distance

Nature didn't create many straight lines. Most of the distances you need to measure on a map are convoluted lines formed by winding trails, streams, roads, and other curvy features. To measure distance along a curved line, use the straight edge of a piece of scrap paper, a mechanical pencil, and the map.

Measuring Distance Along a Curved Line

1. Put the straight-edged paper on the map against the start of the trail you intend to measure. Align the paper with the first section of the trail.

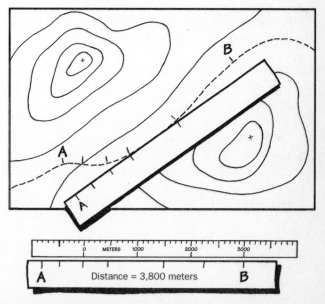

Measuring distance along a curved line

2. Make a slash mark with the pencil, perpendicular to the straight edge and through the start of the trail.

3. Make another perpendicular slash mark from the paper onto the map at the first place where the trail bends away from the paper. (The trail will either bend up and away from the paper's edge or it will disappear underneath.)

4. Keep the second slash mark on the paper and the map lined up and pivot the paper until it is aligned with another section of trail.

5. Make another slash across both the edge of the paper and the map at the next place the trail bends away from the paper. Pivot the paper again until it lines up with the next section of trail. Make another slash. Continue this process until you reach the end of the distance you want to measure.

6. The sum total of the distances marked in pencil on the edge of the paper, from the first slash to the last, is an approximation of the trail's distance.

7. Measure that distance against one of the bar scales at the bottom of your map.

8. Remember again that your approximation will be short of the real-world distance. The more you pivot the paper to make tick marks, the more exact the distance your measurement will be.

NORTH

In order to not confuse map users, mapmakers draw nearly every map with north at the top, usually using the geographic North Pole, the axis about which the earth rotates, as the point lined up with the top of the map. Everybody knows that a compass needle points north, but did you know that your compass does not point to the same north that the top of your map does? It is an unfortunate (and unavoidable) fact that north on your map and north on your compass are not always the same direction. Believe it or not, there are three different kinds of north.

Magnetic North, True North, and Grid North

Compass needles point toward **magnetic north,** which is the location of the "north pole" of the earth's magnetic field. Magnetic north is not in the same place as the geographic North Pole, the axis about which the earth rotates.

North on a topographic map points toward geographic north and is called **true north.**

For most wilderness purposes we can ignore **grid north,** which refers to the top of the Universal Transverse Mercater (UTM) grid that is superimposed on a map to make it quick and easy to assign coordinates to any given point. This grid is an essential feature of military maps (which are oriented to grid north rather than true north), because the military needs a precise and simple method to describe location. Chapter 10 explains how to use the UTM grid.

The difference between true north, magnetic north, and grid north is called **declination,** and it varies from place to place. The declination for each map is found in the marginal information to the left of the bar scales. It looks like a little V, with one line pointing toward true north, and the other toward magnetic north. Depending on the map's location on the globe, the line pointing to magnetic north can either be to the right or left of true north, so look closely.

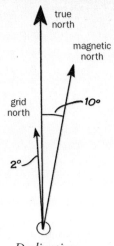

Declination

Declination is often spoken of as, for example, "10 degrees east," which means that magnetic north (where a compass points) is 10 degrees to the right of true north. A declination of "15 degrees west" means that a compass needle points 15 degrees to the left of true north.

There are places in the United States (in the Midwest and South) where true north and magnetic north are the same, but in parts of Alaska the declination angle reaches almost 30 degrees. Don't think you can ignore declination. If you do, someday it will bite you.

MAP CARE

That beautiful new map, so colorful and full of possibility, is doomed. Use it in the field and it'll never be the same—it will get creased, steadily dirtier, smeared, and eventually torn. Use it enough and someday it'll be useless, nothing more than a treasured reminder of past adventure.

Greg's First Law of Navigational Fiascos: The more important any given map location is to your trip, the more likely it will be found at the edge of your map or on a folded, dirty, smeared, wet, or damaged part.

You can slow that inevitable decay by taking proper care of a new map from the minute you buy it. The best way to carry an unfolded map is rolled up inside a cardboard tube. Rolled up and secured with a rubberband is okay if you don't have a cardboard tube, but be careful not to smash the rolled-up map.

If you want your map to last a long time, laminate it. Lamination is an extra cost ($5 to $15) and an extra hassle, but it'll make the thing last a lot longer. It is easier to fold a 1.5mm lamination than a 3mm coating, but 1.5mm is not as durable. If you expect to navigate in the rain, it is a good idea to laminate your maps. A wet map becomes useless in a hurry.

If you're not going to roll your new map and put it in a cardboard tube, take it to a flat, clean surface and fold it. Folded, a map is more portable and less prone to crinkling. Laminated maps can be folded too, just use more force to get crisp creases. Here are two ways to fold a map:

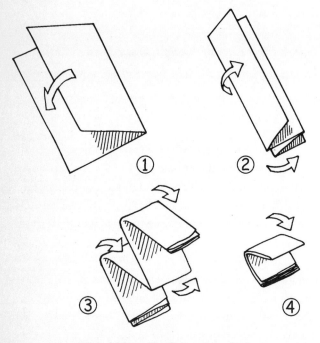

Map folding: Traditional method

For the traditional method, you fold your map from the top edge to bottom edge, fold the edges back to the crease, and finally fold it in half twice. Alternatively, you can use the army method. First, fold the map as in the previous example, so it is divided into 16 squares. Then make a cut and fold as shown below. It certainly takes nerve to cut a brand-new map, but it allows you to flip to the underside of the next fold without resorting to refolding—one of the most damaging events in a map's life.

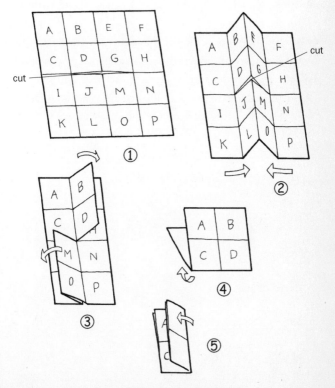

Map folding: Army method

Even lamination won't protect your map 100 percent from water damage—you should still carry it in a plastic bag. You could buy a fancy map case, but none of the cases on the market performs significantly better than a gallon-sized zipper-locked bag. Map cases just cost and weigh more. Bag a folded map with the section you will be traveling across showing through the plastic so you can navigate without taking the map out of the bag. A bagged map stays dry, and sweaty hands do not get it grimy and dirty. If your map gets damp or wet, try not to write on it. Your pencil or pen point will just tear up the surface layer of the map and make it unreadable. Remember—a well-cared-for map stays clean, and a clean map is more accurate and easier to use.

Navigating with Topographic Maps

HOMEWORK

- Study the map of your destination before you leave home. Analyze the terrain. Plan the route you want to take.

- Pinpoint the place on the topographic map where your wilderness journey will start.

- Identify the major terrain features that you'll encounter: rivers, ridges, hills, mountains, passes, etc. Get a feel for the lay of the land.

- Scout your proposed route. Will it be on established trails or cross country? In what general direction will you be traveling? Is there a point where you will be making a major direction change? How many miles away is that direction change? Will you cross any rivers or streams? How many? Where will you be going uphill? Where downhill? Will you be going up a valley toward a pass? Along or across a ridge? How much elevation will you gain? How many miles will you travel each day?

- Put particular effort into planning logical cross-country routes. You can save effort by walking around hills instead of straight over them, and your map can tell you how to do that. Be aware that you may have to adjust your planned cross-country route should you encounter impassable terrain or if you need to minimize your impact on sensitive terrain. See *Leave No Trace* (Falcon 1997) for information on how to minimize your impact on the wilderness.

THE MENTAL PICTURE

Homework is the foundation of your mental picture of the landscape—a picture that is really your sense of direction. Develop it as you travel and add the information you glean from the real world. Be willing to adjust your picture to fit reality if you discover you've made a mistake.

When you arrive at the trailhead, your pack loaded with a week's worth of food and equipment, and you're ready to hit the trail, what do you do to make sure that you won't get lost along the way?

Take out your map and hold it in your hands. Keep it there. Can you pinpoint your location *Right Now* on the large-scale topo you will be using to navigate? If not, take the road map that got you to the trailhead and match the roads that got you there to the same roads on your topo. With the roads identified, you should be able to pinpoint your location. It is sometimes difficult to figure out road networks on a topo because the colors and symbols used for roads on topographic maps are different from the ones used for road maps. Next, **orient** your map—align the map to the features of the real world.

HOW TO ORIENT A MAP

There are two ways to orient a map—without and with a compass. These methods are not mutually exclusive. It's a good idea to combine both techniques to double-check yourself.

Where long vistas are common, you should be able to orient your map without a compass using visible terrain. In forests, swamps, jungles, whiteouts, or at night, however, it can be difficult or impossible to discern north from the other directions or to see distant terrain features. In such circumstances, use a compass to orient the map.

How to Orient a Map Without a Compass

1. Hold your folded map in front of you so that you can see your map location through the plastic (your map should be neatly folded and stashed in a zipper-locked bag as discussed in the "Map Care" section of Chapter 2).

2. Can you find your exact location on the map? When you do, can you identify which way is north? Take clues from the landscape and from your prior study of the map. Can you see a major river or mountain range that runs from north to south? Is it early morning or late evening? Check the sun—it rises in the east and sets in the west.

3. If you can identify north, you can orient the map right away. Hold your folded map face-up in front of your chest with north at the top, and pivot your entire body until you face north. You and your map are now oriented.

4. If you cannot identify north (without a compass), use a feature in the landscape to help. Look up at the real world and pick out a prominent terrain feature—a hill or mountain, a long ridge, a bend in a river or stream, etc., then locate that feature on the map. Twist your body and map so your current map location and the map position of the terrain feature you've just identified match up with their real-world alignment. When your map is aligned to the real world, north is the direction indicated by the top of the map—and your map is oriented.

How to Orient a Map with a Compass

1. To orient a map with a compass, you must line up north on the map with north on the compass. Remember that true north and magnetic north are different—and that the difference between the two varies depending on where you are on the earth's surface. To orient your map correctly, you must account for that difference. Find the local declination in your map's marginal information. There are three possibilities: Magnetic north is to the left of true north, magnetic north is to the right of true north, or magnetic north and true north are the same.

   If you have a baseplate compass, you can adjust the baseplate to compensate for declination and the compass will "remember" the local declination. Offset the orienting arrow from N (on the compass's rotating case) by the amount of the declination, either to the left or right of N.

2. Put your compass on the map and carefully line up one of the long sides of the baseplate with a true north line on the map—the left or right margin or any other line of longitude will work.

3. Rotate the map and compass together until the compass needle sits within the orienting arrow. (The compass needle still points toward magnetic north—that's the only thing it *can* do—but you have adjusted the orienting arrow and the rotating case to compensate for declination.)

4. When everything is properly lined up—baseplate edge to a true north line on the map and the compass needle neatly within the orienting arrow, the map is oriented to true north. Refer to the illustration below.

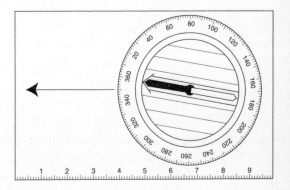

A baseplate compass set at 10 degrees of declination

If you don't have a baseplate compass that you can adjust to compensate for declination, here is a way to improvise:

- If magnetic north is east (right) of map north, let the compass needle point to the number that is the number of degrees of the declination; i.e., if the declination is 13 degrees east, let the needle point to 13 degrees. Then 0 degrees points to true north.
- If magnetic north is west (left) of north, let the compass needle point to the number that is 360 degrees minus the number of degrees of declination; i.e., if the declination is 13 degrees west, let the needle point to 360-13=347 degrees. Then 0 degrees points to true north.
- With the compass needle pointing to the correct number to account for the declination, align a true north line on your map with the line between 0 and 180 degrees on your compass and the map is oriented.

To keep yourself from having to check every time, affix a small triangle of tape to the compass dial at the degree mark that corresponds to the local declination. For example, if the declination is 26 degrees east, as it is in parts of the Alaska Range, attach a tiny triangle of white tape to the dial at 26 degrees east. When the compass needle points to the piece of tape, the line between 0 degrees and 180 degrees on the compass dial points at true north. When the declination is to the west of true north, subtract the number of degrees of the declination from 360 (the same as 0 degrees because there are 360 degrees in a circle) and affix the piece of tape to the appropriate number. Therefore, if the declination in the area you will be traveling is 7 degrees west of true north, subtract 7 from 360 and affix the tape at 353 degrees. Align a true north line on the map with the line between 0 degrees and 180 degrees on the compass. Rotate the map and compass together until the compass needle points to the piece of tape and your map is oriented.

If you don't have a baseplate compass and don't want to use the tape trick, just let the compass needle point to the correct number of degrees to account for declination.

Keep Your Map Oriented at All Times

- When you change the direction that you are facing, change the way you hold the map.
- If you look west, hold your map so that you look over the western edge of your map. The eastern edge should be closest to your chest and the western edge away from your body, toward the terrain in the distance. When you look west, north is to your right, so the western edge of the map should be away from your body.
- If you look east, hold your map so that you look over the map's eastern edge.
- When you look south, hold the map so that you look over the map's southern edge. Southwest? Northeast? Do the same. As you change the direction that you are looking, rotate the map so that the map stays oriented to the real world it represents.

Caution: Use both terrain association and your compass to orient your map (especially when you are learning) and you will not make a mistake. Misorienting the map is a BIG mistake, one sure to get you lost.

HOW TO NAVIGATE USING TERRAIN ASSOCIATION

Terrain association combines your mental picture of what the unseen landscape should look like with what the real world actually does look like. The map is the bridge linking the two pictures as you travel. **Keep your map oriented at all times.** If you can do this correctly as you travel, you'll never get utterly lost, just occasionally confused—and that is an enormous difference. As you travel, be aware of your surroundings—what's ahead, as well as what's behind. **Constantly develop your mental picture** of the landscape. Study the lay of the land. Keep your map oriented to whatever direction you are facing—as you turn, turn the map. Find the features on the map that you can see in the real world. Relate the terrain around you to your current position. Locate where you are *Right Now* on the map. Small fluctuations in contour lines allow you to pinpoint your location with surprising accuracy. This takes practice, but you will improve as you become more experienced. Use the information provided by the map's colors, symbols, and contours to visualize the terrain of your upcoming journey.

This is the heart of navigation: Keep your map oriented and relate the real world and the map world in both directions, from map to terrain and from terrain to map. Pinpoint your position on the map. Visualize the terrain ahead and know where you are.

TERRAIN ASSOCIATION STEP BY STEP

1. Orient the map to the direction you are facing.

2. Identify major terrain features in the distance and the minor features in your immediate vicinity.

3. Match those features to their representations on the map.

4. Pinpoint your location *Right Now* in relation to those major and minor features.

5. Identify where you want to go.

6. Know what to expect from the terrain ahead.

7. As you travel, examine the terrain through which you are traveling and chart your progress on the map.

8. As soon as things in the real world don't match up with what you expect, STOP. You are in danger of becoming lost. Take the time to pinpoint your location. Figure out what terrain or map feature deceived you.

9. Keep oriented to the terrain around you and know where you are *Right Now*.

◖ NAVIGATION TIPS

Don't point at the map with your finger; it is 500 meters wide on the map. Point with a pencil lead, a blade of grass, a twig, a pine needle, a knife point—anything with a point, but not with your finger. Navigation is all about precision and a 500-meter-wide finger is not a precision instrument.

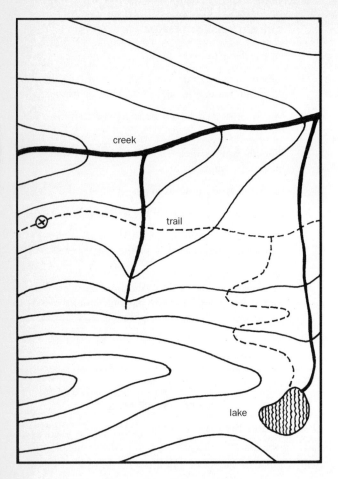

Illustration of map analysis

Know your basic direction of travel and glance at your compass occasionally to verify that you are, in fact, traveling in that direction.

Determine from the map what your next landmark will be and use it to chart your progress, be it a trail junction, stream crossing, saddle, switchback, or any other terrain you can positively identify both on the ground and on the map.

Here is an example of the mental process that goes into analyzing the map as you navigate (refer to the map on page 42): "Okay, the map shows that the trail stays on this side of the valley. I should contour around the face of a broad ridge. Past the ridge I cross a stream that descends from right to left. There should be a trail junction about 500 meters past the stream. I want the right fork. If I cross a second stream, then I've gone too far and missed the trail junction. The right fork goes up a set of steep switchbacks to the northern shore of a small lake, and that's where I want to spend the night."

Note how the preceding example uses the second stream crossing to warn of an error. Use the map to create such "restraining lines" to prevent minor errors (such as missing a trail junction) from turning into major ones. A **restraining line** is any terrain feature that you use to limit your advance. Any easily recognizable terrain feature can be used as a restraining line: a stream or river, a ridgeline or lake, etc.

THE BOTTOM LINE

Can you pinpoint your location *Right Now?* If so, you are doing fine.

Navigating with an Altimeter

Altimeters can be valuable navigational tools. Since contour lines allow you to figure the elevation of any point on a topographic map, you can use your known elevation to help pinpoint your exact location. An altimeter is particularly useful when you're navigating in a steep, mountainous area. With an altimeter you can chart your vertical progress to about plus or minus 300 feet. Here's how it works:

Let's say you're climbing a long, steep mountain ridge. You know what ridge you are on, but you don't know exactly where. Your altimeter says that you're at 9,350 feet.

The map's contour interval is 100 feet. Find the 9,000-foot index contour line and count up 100 feet for every contour line above 9,000 feet until you hit the 9,300-foot contour line. You are located on the ridge between the 9,300- and 9,400-foot contour lines. Since the mountain you are climbing is 11,400 feet high, you've got just over 2,000 feet to go to the top.

A good altimeter is a sensitive instrument that measures the current atmospheric pressure and translates that information into an elevation reading. But atmospheric pressure fluctuates as the weather changes, so an altimeter will display varying elevations even when it doesn't physically move up or down. What really changes is the weight of the air over the altimeter. Typically, when the weather is good, the atmospheric pressure is high, and an altimeter will indicate an elevation less than its actual elevation. Conversely, when the weather is bad, the atmospheric pressure is usually low, and an altimeter will indicate an elevation above its actual elevation.

Don't expect the instrument to be more accurate than plus or minus 300 feet, because powerful storms or strong high pressure systems can make altimeters swing up to 1,000 feet. Normal fluctuations cause an altimeter to bounce up and down several hundred feet. However, an altimeter will give you an idea of your distance above sea level, and you can use that figure to help fix your position. You can increase the accuracy of your altimeter by adjusting the device to a known elevation at every opportunity. Maps often show the exact elevation of lakes, passes, and summits, and you can set your altimeter to that elevation when you are standing there.

Navigating with a Compass

The compass is a support tool. The essence of wilderness navigation is to know how to read and interpret a map, but a compass is a powerful aid, and in certain situations a compass and knowledge of how to use it are absolutely critical to accurate navigation.

You can easily spend an entire week off trail in the wilderness and know exactly where you are at all times without resorting to a compass, but heavily forested terrain makes terrain association difficult and a compass much more important. In certain circumstances—jungle travel, hiking at night, or in a storm or winter whiteout—you will not be able to navigate accurately without one.

Trust your compass. The north-seeking needle of your compass is one of the few truly reliable devices. Unless a magnetic disturbance (e.g., a big chunk of metal) is interfering, a compass does not lie. Don't use your compass on the hood of your car or hold two next to each other—they'll affect each other's reading.

What a compass does: The needle points to magnetic north and the degree marks around the dial measure the angle clockwise from magnetic north to any other given direction. Azimuth, heading, and bearing are all words that mean direction. Direction is the angle measured clockwise from a northern base point. To complicate matters, the northern base point could be true north, grid north, or magnetic north. When you measure or plot direction, make sure to use the right kind of north (see the discussion of "North" in Chapter 2). When you compare two directions, make sure that you compare magnetic to magnetic directions or true to true directions, or you will end up in a classic apples-and-oranges situation.

Caution: *It is possible to confuse north and south on a compass in an emergency situation. Don't panic. Be extra careful to double-check your readings.*

What a Compass Can Do for You When You Don't Have a Map

- Help you travel in a straight line.
- Help you reverse that line and return to your starting point.
- Tell you what direction to travel toward some distant landmark. The compass will keep you traveling in that direction even when you can't see the landmark.
- Help you find a restraining line, provided you know what side of the line you are on.
- If you can keep track of your direction (or directions) of travel, you can reverse direction(s) and return to your starting point.

How to Measure the Direction to a Distant Landmark

1. Hold the compass face up in front of your chest.
2. Face the landmark.
3. Let the compass needle come to rest. It now points to magnetic north.
4. Line up the needle with the zero-degree mark on the rotating case and the orienting arrow at the bottom of the compass housing.
5. Rotate the baseplate underneath the case until the front sight and the direction-of-travel line point at the landmark.
6. Note the number of degrees on the rotating case behind the front sight. This is the direction you need to travel to reach the landmark.
7. Leave your compass's baseplate adjusted toward your direction of travel.

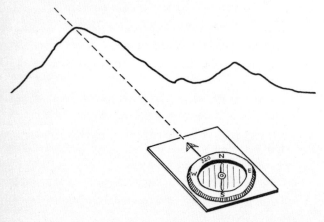

Measuring the direction to a distant landmark

It is hard for the human animal to walk in a straight line, but a compass makes it possible to do just that. However, just because you know a specific bearing to a far-off point is no guarantee that you will, in fact, walk in a straight line. A direction can be any one of an infinite number of parallel lines.

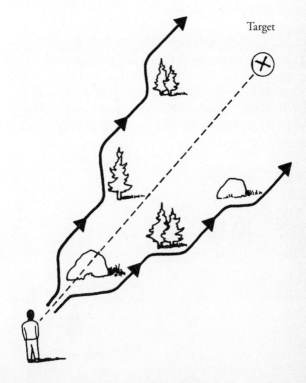

Target

Lateral drift

HOW TO WALK A STRAIGHT LINE

To ensure that you are walking a straight line, you need to sight to a specific intermediate point on your heading and move to it. Once you get to that intermediate point, sight along your chosen direction again and pick out another intermediate point and move to it. Repeat this process until you arrive at your objective.

How to Sight to an Intermediate Point

1. Hold your compass in front of your chest and let the needle align with the north arrow and the 0-degree mark on the dial. The direction-of-travel line and the front sight indicate your direction of travel (if your compass is still adjusted to that direction from the steps on page 48).

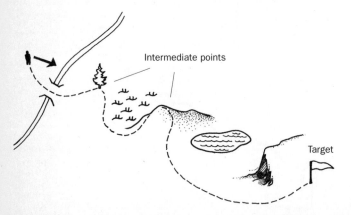

Using intermediate points to get around an obstacle

2. Look along the sighting line and pick out something in the landscape that is on that line—a stone, a tree, or anything else that isn't going to move.

3. Walk to that point and repeat the process.

This intermediate point process stops you from drifting from side to side and keeps you to the one specific line you originally intended. It also allows you to detour around obstacles and return to the original line.

HOW TO REVERSE DIRECTION

Since degrees measure distinct points around a circle, you can reverse your direction of travel and return to your starting point at any time. These reverse directions are often called back azimuths, back bearings, reciprocal bearings, or reciprocal directions.

How To Calculate a Reverse Direction

1. If your direction of travel is between 0 and 180 degrees: Add 180 degrees to your direction of travel. **Current direction + 180 = reverse direction.** If your direction of travel is between 180 and 360 degrees: Subtract 180 degrees from your direction of travel. **Current direction – 180 = reverse direction.**

2. Set your baseplate sighting line to the reverse direction and follow it (using intermediate points as detailed above) to return to your starting point.

If you carefully record all your directions, and note the location of each direction change you make, you can retrace your route by calculating the reverse directions for each leg. Double-check your arithmetic before you begin the return journey.

If you've been wandering aimlessly in the woods, to the east of a river or stream, you can find your way back to the river by looking at your compass and traveling west until you hit the river. This trick works with a road, trail, ridge, or any other linear terrain feature that can be used as a restraining line.

The ability to travel in a straight line becomes an even more effective navigational weapon if you know the distance you travel along that straight line. The best way to know how far you've traveled in the wilderness is to use your pace count.

USING YOUR PACE COUNT TO ESTIMATE DISTANCE

1. Find a track near your home. (One where human athletes train—not a dog or horse track.)
2. Stand with both feet on the starting line for the 100-meter dash.
3. Step forward with your left foot first and walk comfortably, like you would hiking. Count one pace each time your right foot strikes the ground until you arrive at the 100-meter finish line. Write the number of paces down.
4. Repeat the process three or four times and average the results. This is your pace count (per hundred meters).

Kilometers are much easier to use than miles because of the base-ten nature of the metric system. But if you are more comfortable with miles, use a football field to pace off 100 yards and remember that there are 17.6 100-yard lengths in a mile. U.S. Geological Survey (USGS) topographic maps have bar scales for both miles and kilometers, so take your pick. Maps made in any country other than the United States will only have metric measurements.

You will take more paces in the wilderness to cover the same 100-meter distance than you did on the track because your stride gets shorter as the terrain gets more difficult. Add 10 percent to your track pace count for even the most simple wilderness terrain. Traveling up steep broken slopes, through snow, at night, or during strenuous bushwhacking, you will find that your pace count is nearly double (or even more) what it was on the track. Seize any opportunity to calculate your pace count for a known distance over broken terrain.

This pace count shift is a "feel" thing, and the only way to get a good idea of how terrain and conditions affect your pace is to practice in the real world.

🔘 NAVIGATION TIP

Find ten small pebbles. Put them all in one pocket. Every time you pace off 100 meters, transfer one pebble to another pocket. When you've moved all ten pebbles to the new pocket, you've gone one kilometer. Put the pebbles back in the original pocket (this will stop you from forgetting which way you are moving the pebbles) and repeat the process. For distances in miles, use 17 pebbles to count off one mile (17.6 x 100 yards = 1 mile).

Dead-Reckoning Navigation

Navigating with map, compass, and pace count when you can't see the distant landscape (and therefore can't use terrain association) is called dead reckoning. Dead reckoning is a critical navigation technique in dense forest, jungle, swamp, at night, in a storm, or in a whiteout—situations when terrain association is difficult or impossible.

When dead reckoning, you calculate the precise distance and direction you must travel from the map. Remember that when you calculate a direction from the map, it will be a "true direction" (based on true north), and you *must* change that true direction to a magnetic direction before you can use it on a compass, which can only measure magnetic directions. (See page 28 for a review of declination.)

Before you can begin to calculate a course from the map, you must know the exact spot where you plan to begin dead reckoning. That can either be your current location or some specific landmark you will reach using terrain association.

How to Calculate a Dead-reckoning Course

1. Locate the beginning and end points of each leg of the journey on the map and mark them.

2. Connect the beginning and end points of each leg with a straight line.

3. Measure the straight-line distance of each leg.

4. Measure the direction of each leg using a protractor or with a baseplate compass (see pages 57 and 58). These directions will be true-north directions, so don't use them on your compass without first converting them to magnetic directions.

5. Convert the true-north directions calculated in step 4 to magnetic directions.

6. Make a list of the direction and distance you will travel for each leg of the journey. Include any topographic details about each leg and the end point that will help your navigation.

Don't trust your memory. Write down the distance and magnetic heading for each leg. Make all the marks on your map with the fine-point mechanical pencil in your navigator's kit. And check, check, and double-check your calculations.

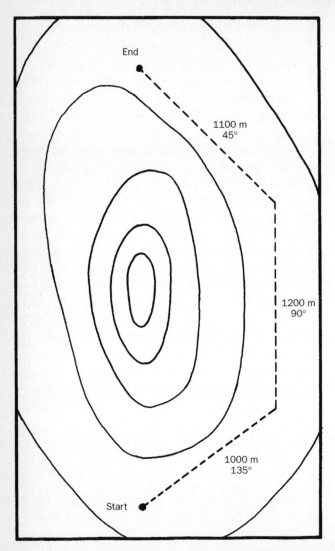

End

1100 m
45°

1200 m
90°

1000 m
135°

Start

A dead-reckoning course with multiple legs

How to Measure Direction on the Map with a Protractor

1. Extend the straight line that goes from the beginning to the end of the leg whose direction you want to calculate so that it is longer than the radius of your protractor. Otherwise, you won't be able to read the protractor accurately. Accuracy when measuring direction is critical.

2. Put the X in the center of your protractor anywhere on that line.

3. Line up the zero-degree mark on the protractor with true north (the top of the map, also called map north).

The number of degrees where the line of direction for the leg intersects the protractor is the map direction of the leg. *Do not* measure the opposite direction from the way you intend to travel, which would give you a reverse direction and would lead to a major navigational fiasco.

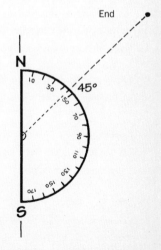

How to calculate a true-north direction with a protractor

How to Measure Direction on the Map
With a Baseplate Compass

1. Draw a line with a straightedge that connects the beginning and end points of the leg whose direction you want to calculate.

2. Ignore the compass needle. You are using the compass as a protractor in this operation. This has nothing to do with magnetic north.

3. Put the compass baseplate against the line you just drew. Make sure the direction-of-travel line points in the direction that you will travel along the line.

4. Twist the compass housing within the baseplate until the orienting lines in the compass housing are aligned with true north (or grid north—see Chapter 10 if using a UTM grid).

5. Note the number of degrees where the direction-of-travel line intersects the 360-degree compass dial. This is the map direction you intend to travel.

6. Even though you used your baseplate compass to measure the direction (relative to true north), you must still convert it to a magnetic direction before you can use it to navigate with the compass.

Remember, before you can use the map direction you just measured to navigate with your compass, you *must* convert it to a magnetic direction.

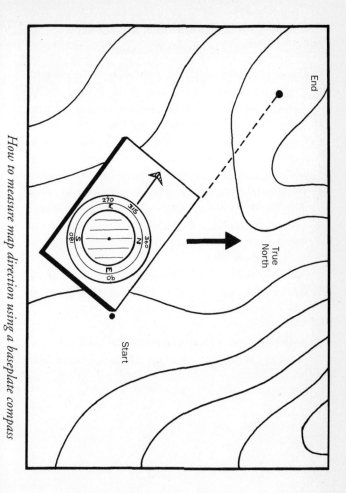

How to measure map direction using a baseplate compass

How to Convert a Measured Map Direction to a Magnetic Direction

1. Consult the map's declination diagram in the margin.
2. If magnetic north is left (west) of true north, *add* the declination to the true-north direction to convert a true-north direction to a magnetic direction.
3. If magnetic north is right (east) of true north, *subtract* the declination from the true-north direction to convert a true-north direction to a magnetic direction.
4. The simple sketch below makes it obvious whether you should add or subtract. Make it for each angle and you won't make a crucial error. Double-check your calculations before you commit to traveling your converted magnetic directions.
5. Calculate the magnetic direction for each leg of the journey and enter the result into the list of direction and distance for each leg.

A simple rhyme to help you remember this:
"Map to magnetic, it's a fact, left add and right subtract."

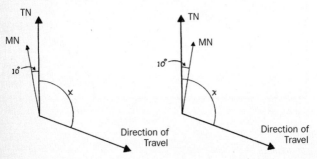

Left add, right subtract

PLANNING A DEAD-RECKONING ROUTE

The thought process that goes into planning each individual leg of a dead-reckoning course is very important. When you plan to dead reckon, you usually can't just draw a straight line between where you are now and where you want to go. A straight line between those two points might go over a cliff, through a swamp or lake, up and over a big hill, or across other terrain that you want to avoid. Study your map to see if there are any obstacles on the line between you and your destination. If there are no obstacles, great! Calculate the magnetic direction and distance you need to travel and away you go. More likely, there will be difficult terrain between you and your destination, which will force you to plot a course with several direction changes. Analyze the map and decide what is the best route to take.

Note how the example on the following page includes two more direction changes than the straight-line course, but the three-legged option avoids the hilltop and swamp.

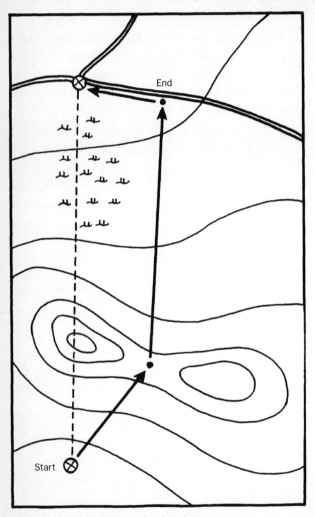

Planning a dead-reckoning route

AVOID MISTAKES WITH MAP ANALYSIS

- Does each leg go uphill or downhill? If the map shows a leg as only going downhill, then you should get suspicious if you encounter an up-slope larger than the contour interval. (Remember that an up-slope with less vertical change than the contour interval won't appear on the map.)
- Does the leg go up and over a ridge? If so, you have confirmation of the progress you are making along the straight line when you start to go downhill.
- Does the leg cross a linear terrain feature like a stream, road, or trail? If so, when you encounter that feature you'll know what distance you have traveled.

The potential for error is greatest at the end of each leg. Aim to make your direction changes from a spot that you can pinpoint precisely using terrain association. The closer you are to the *exact location* of the map point from which you calculated the next direction and distance, the more accurate your dead reckoning will be. Use a recognizable terrain feature for the beginning and end points of each leg and you will be able to correct for errors in precision that you might make and prevent errors from compounding.

Remember, hilltops, saddles, stream junctions, or any other obvious terrain feature can give you a precise position fix. In addition, your pace count will tell you when you are near the end of a leg and when you should encounter the exact terrain feature you chose at the beginning of the next leg.

THE CALCULATED MISS

Let's say that you are navigating in a dense forest and plan to make your next direction change at a stream junction—a location that you can pinpoint both on the map and in the real world. Do not plot a course directly to the junction. If you aim directly for the junction and you arrive at the stream, but not at the junction, you won't know whether you are upstream or downstream of the junction.

However, if you go for the "calculated miss" (often called "aiming off"), and intentionally aim for a point a few hundred meters up or downstream of the junction, when you arrive at the stream you will *know* which way to turn. All you have to do is walk in that direction until you reach the junction. Another advantage of this technique is that you don't have to maintain an exact pace count. It's enough to know that you are approaching the correct stream. The exact distance of the leg isn't critical if you have an obvious **restraining line** to limit your advance. Just be sure to plot the next leg of your journey from the stream junction, not from where your original heading intersected the stream.

When you start incorporating this level of map analysis, terrain association, and dead reckoning into your navigation, you are becoming truly skilled. Be aware that a stream that the map shows as perennial might be intermittent and not have any water in it when you get there. Even if there is no water, you should still be able to identify the streambed.

Once you've planned and prepared your dead-reckoning course, you are ready to go.

TRAVELING USING DEAD RECKONING

Use these skills to ensure that you successfully reach your destination when dead reckoning:

- Set a heading on the compass.
- Travel a straight line on a specific heading and maintain a pace count.
- Bypass an obstacle and maintain the pace count.

How to Set a Heading on a Baseplate Compass

1. Use the magnetic direction you calculated when planning your dead-reckoning course.
2. Hold your baseplate compass flat.
3. Twist the baseplate until the direction-of-travel line is aligned with the magnetic direction you intend to travel.

Use the same techniques for straight-line travel that you learned in the "How to Walk a Straight Line" section on page 50. Maintain your pace count as you travel.

You will encounter obstacles that you cannot plow through when traveling a specific heading and trying to keep an accurate pace count. If you haphazardly deviate around an obstacle, you will lose the precision of your pace count. Here's how to avoid that obstacle and maintain the count:

How to Bypass an Obstacle and Maintain Your Pace Count

1. Stop short of the obstacle.

2. Write down your current pace count.

3. Decide whether it is easier to go left or right around the obstacle.

4. Make a 90-degree turn to either the left or right. Adjust your compass so that you head exactly 90-degrees from your course. If you make a **right turn, add 90 degrees** to your heading. If the number is larger than 360 degrees, subtract 360 and use that heading. For example, 347+90=437; 437−360=77. Travel the 77-degree heading. If you make a **left turn, subtract 90 degrees** from your current heading. If your current heading is less than 90 degrees, you will end up with a negative number. Subtract the number of degrees less than 0 from 360 and use that heading. For example, 53−90=−37; 360−37=323. Travel the 323-degree heading.

5. Count paces as you walk the course at right angles to your direction of travel.

6. When you have gone far enough on the right angle course to avoid the obstacle, stop.

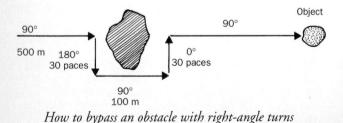

How to bypass an obstacle with right-angle turns

7. Write down the number of paces you took away from your original line of travel.

8. Reset your compass to your original heading.

9. Travel a straight line on your original heading, adding to your original pace count. When you have gone past the obstacle, write down your total pace count. Make a 90-degree turn back toward your original line of travel.

10. Pace off the distance back to the original line of travel.

11. Reset your compass to the original heading and continue on your way, adding to the total pace count you arrived at in step 9.

Keep track of all your headings and the distance that you travel on each heading. Those notes will allow you to retrace your steps to your beginning point by traveling the same distance in the reverse direction of each leg.

Finding Yourself

Greg's Second Law of Navigational Fiascos: If you've been lost, and you manage to figure out exactly where you are, there will be a big hill between where you are right now and where you need to be.

So, you don't know where you are *Right Now*? That ugly, uncertain feeling has grabbed your guts? Confused and scared? First, *Stop, Think,* and *Relax.* Make a coherent plan of action to get found or else you might find yourself wandering around in circles—perhaps literally.

- Orient the map with your compass (because it won't lie).
- Can you relate the oriented map to the terrain around you and locate your position?
- Where was the last point that you were certain of your location? Can you relate that last point to your current location?
- Can you retrace your steps to that last place where you were certain of your location?

That was just a little case of disorientation, and not a big deal. But someday you might find that you have been traveling for a long time when you suddenly realize that you have absolutely no idea where you are. You are completely and utterly lost. Again, *Stop, Think, Relax,* and maybe laugh.

- Orient the map with your compass.
- Study the terrain features on the map and try and relate them to the terrain around you. Do any of those terrain features you can see conform to something on the map? If so, double-check your reasoning. It's very easy to convince yourself that what you see conforms to what you have on the map. The fit must be exact—otherwise you *do not* know where you are. What type of terrain are you on or in right now? A valley or draw? A ridge or spur? A forest? Alongside a stream? Use all available clues to limit the scope of your search for identifiable terrain on the map.
- Do you at least know what general direction you've been traveling from your beginning point? Try to find something to limit the scope of area where you might be.
- Can you improve your view of the surrounding landscape by climbing a hill, ridge, or tree in the immediate area? A good view can help.
- If you can't locate yourself after much effort, can you retrace your steps?
- Do you know if you're to one side of a major linear **restraining line** like a river or road? Say you're on the north slope of the Wind River Mountains, but you have no idea where—go northeast far enough and you will certainly bump into a major highway. But that is a last resort that will wreck your trip.
- Can you specifically identify one or two far-off terrain feature(s)? If so, you can do a **resection** to nail down your location.

If you can identify one far-off terrain feature, such as a mountain, you can calculate the line on which you are located. If you can identify two or more distant terrain features, you can pinpoint your exact location. Here's how:

RESECTION

1. Use your compass to measure the exact magnetic direction from you to a distant terrain feature that you have pinpointed on the map.
2. Convert that magnetic direction to a true north direction.
3. Calculate the **true north reverse direction** of the true north direction.
4. Put your protractor on the exact map location that you sighted to with your compass and line up zero degrees on the protractor with north on the map.
5. Mark the reverse direction from the distant landmark on the map and draw a line with a straight edge and mechanical pencil from the targeted terrain feature and through the mark. Draw a long line. *You are located somewhere on that line.* Double-check your calculations.

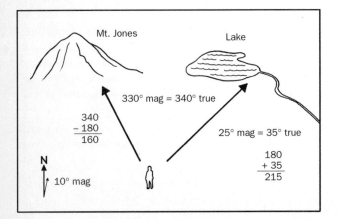

Taking bearings for resection

Can you identify a second distant feature? If so, sight the magnetic direction to it and repeat the above instructions. You are located where the two lines intersect. Repeat the process with a third distant landmark to confirm your work. If there is a large difference between the points of intersection, check your calculations—you made a mistake.

For a **resection** to work, you must be *absolutely certain* of the distant landmark's location on the map. Be careful when using hill and mountaintops as points of resection because what you see might not actually be the true summit.

If you are on or alongside a linear terrain feature like a trail, river, stream, or ridgeline, but don't know exactly where, you can pinpoint your location with just one line of resection. You are located where the resection line intersects the linear terrain feature.

Remember to *think* when you are lost or disoriented.

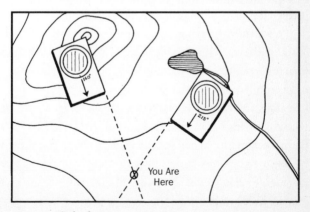

Calculating your position using resection

Special Navigation Situations

Do not underestimate the navigational challenges presented by whiteouts, storms, jungles, dense forests, deserts, or darkness. These environments and circumstances demand total concentration. And the consequences of getting lost in extreme environments are worse. The elements are more savage and it is harder for rescuers to locate lost individuals.

WINTER

Following a trail covered with a foot of fresh snow is not easy. An early-season dump can turn a casual hike on a well-used trail into a complex navigational challenge.

With snow covering the ground you can't blithely follow a trail—you won't be able to see it. Winter forces you to use cross-country–style terrain association, dead reckoning, or a combination of both techniques. The trees next to popular trails are sometimes marked with blazes, eye-level scars where the bark has been stripped from tree trunks to leave permanent marks. When you stand at one blaze you should be able to see another farther along the trail. Sometimes there are cut logs along an established trail that will indicate that you are indeed still on the trail.

In the dead of winter it can even be hard to identify lakes—they will be frozen and look like the rest of the landscape, complete with a bumpy surface caused by drifting snow. Streams also blend in when they're filled with snow. Strong winter winds can cause a ground-level whiteout, and blowing snow can play havoc with your terrain association, so have a compass plan as a backup.

WHITEOUTS

Those gently falling flakes didn't seem like a big deal when you curled up in the tent last night, and the noise faded as you drifted off to sleep. But you woke up this morning and everything is white. The snow is piled up on the tent, yesterday's tracks in the snow are totally buried, and visibility through the blizzard is down to about 25 meters. Trouble.

Whiteout navigation is the greatest daytime navigational challenge. Keep your wits about you. Don't get confused in a world of swirling snow. Long-range terrain association is impossible—you can only get terrain association clues from the terrain you are currently standing on. Sound planning and thinking are crucial to success. Once you get disoriented in a whiteout it is often impossible to retrace your steps as the blowing and falling snow obscures your tracks.

- Do you have to travel today? If not, don't. No whiteout lasts forever. Wait. But perhaps you're just out for a day's backcountry ski, aren't equipped for a night out, and you must get back to the car.

- Make a solid navigational plan. Make it simple, with as few direction changes as possible.
- You'll be most successful if you aim for obvious linear terrain features (restraining lines), like major roads that cut across your direction of travel at right angles. Make a plan like: "Head downhill and generally west for about 5 kilometers until I hit a hard-surface road. Turn right and follow the road until I get to the parking lot."
- The storm will play havoc with your pace count, and a pair of skis will make it nonfunctional, so plan a series of recognizable restraining lines that cut across your path to tell you when you are near an objective and when you have gone too far.
- Plan your direction changes to take place at obvious terrain features.
- Use the clues that you glean from the terrain you travel over to confirm your position: always downhill or uphill, a change in slope, a ravine you must cut across, etc.

JUNGLE AND DENSE FOREST

The "greenout." Jungle navigation is a lot like whiteout navigation because you must rely primarily on dead reckoning and can only use clues from terrain association to confirm your progress.

- It is extremely easy to get lost in the jungle. You just can't see far enough for terrain association.
- Dead reckoning is your best navigational option. Trust your compass and pace count.
- You can trust the major terrain features on the map, the scale, and the relative positions of the major terrain, but

don't trust small terrain features. Most jungle maps are made from radar images and aerial photos, not from actual surveying on the ground. The top of the jungle canopy is often what gets mapped, not the ground. Map inaccuracies are legion. Pay particular attention to your pace count, as distance and direction traveled from the last known point is often the most precise way to fix your position.

- An effective time-saving method for passing the myriad obstacles in the jungle is to pass one tree on the left, the next on the right, the next on the left, and so forth. This isn't very precise, but it should average out to zero net lateral drift. This technique adds a few paces to your pace count.

- Examine the map and plan a **panic direction.** Think: "Okay, from anywhere in this region, I can travel due south and hit that road (or river, or coastline, or any re-straining line) if I get lost."

- Remember to "aim off" (the calculated miss technique, see page 64) in the jungle when heading toward a linear terrain feature like a road or stream.

DESERT

Deserts seem like they ought to be easy places to navigate. They're not. Eyeballing distances in deserts is very hard to do—you will almost always underestimate, and much desert terrain does not rise out of the desert—it sinks into it. Wadis, washes, ravines, and canyons cut into the desert floor. Many of the features are small enough to sneak between the con-tour interval. This means that major desert terrain "hides" from you until you literally stumble onto it. You are left to sort out the problems of the minor terrain.

The **resection** (see page 70) is a staple of desert navigation because it is often difficult to sort out the minor terrain features in your immediate vicinity. Fortunately, you can usually see a mountain range, a line of hills, or some mesas in the distance. Do a resection from those identifiable terrain features to fix your position.

Beware of trails and dirt roads on old maps. Roads and trails seem to shift with the desert winds and may not be accurately located on the map—even if the map is only a few years old. Make sure you've got enough water before venturing into the desert. A day or two without water in the desert and the vultures will pick your bones clean.

NIGHT

Navigation is much more difficult at night. A dark night makes open terrain as difficult to navigate as the jungle. All of the principles of terrain association and dead reckoning still apply, but you must prepare more and pay more attention to detail.

- Carefully plan your route ahead of time.
- Use a detailed combination of both terrain association and dead reckoning to keep track of your location *Right Now*. Concentrate.

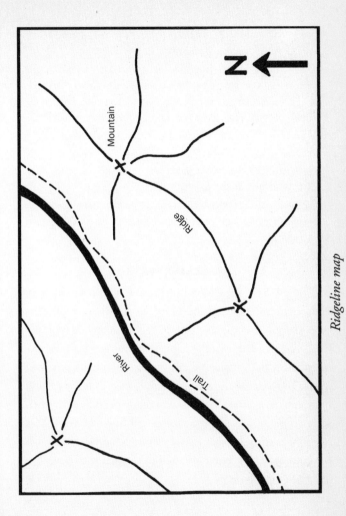

Ridgeline map

- Study the map carefully before moving at night and commit as much detail to memory as possible.
- If you use your flashlight a lot it will affect your night vision and you won't be able to see the shapes of the landscape to use for terrain association. A red filter over your flashlight will let you use the light and preserve your vision.
- It is difficult to judge distance visually in the dark.
- A large feature in the distance will obscure terrain in the foreground at night because you can't see the silhouette of the terrain in the foreground.
- When you terrain associate at night, use compass bearings and pace counts as a backup to your terrain association.

RIDGELINE MAPS

You might have to use one of these maps to navigate in mountainous regions of the Third World where wilderness areas are not carefully mapped. Ridgeline maps are typically small scale and show only significant terrain features like mountains, hills, major ridges, passes, valleys, glaciers, and rivers. You can use these maps to find major objectives and for rough navigation. The precision that is possible with large-scale topographic maps is not possible when you use a ridgeline map, but you can chart your rough progress through the landscape by staying oriented to the major terrain. (See illustration on page 77.)

Following Trails

Use has filled the modern wilderness with trails. Trail signs and maintained trails take a little of the "wild" out of the wilderness, but they are necessary due to the volume of human traffic in the wilderness these days. Use them! Don't spread the damage caused by too many feet.

WELL-ESTABLISHED TRAILS

Following a well-established trail is a straightforward endeavor, but chart your progress on the map anyway. Use the opportunity to improve your terrain association skill with little risk. You won't have to worry much about getting lost when you are on a good trail. Make sure each junction you pass is on the map, so you know where you are if trail markers are stolen or vandalized. Also, make sure you start at the right trailhead; starting at the wrong trailhead can really mess you up.

FAINT TRAILS

Staying on a faint trail is a route-finding skill that complements your map reading and land navigation. Not all trails in the backcountry are well defined. Trails that don't get much use gradually return to their wild state, but they leave clues that help you follow them. Here are a few tips that can help you stay on the trail as you head toward your destination:

- Be aware of the trail and where it's taking you.
- The depiction of the trail on the map will tell you where the trail ought to be, so if a faint trail deviates from where the map tells you it ought to go, maybe it is you who is deviating from the trail.
- Trails are usually logical. If the trail seems to be doing something weird, maybe it is you who is doing something weird.
- If a faint trail seems to be fading out, stop, think, and check the map. Does your map confirm that the trail ought to be where you are right now?
- Look around—did you just miss a turn?
- Look back and examine the trail behind you—is that really a trail?
- If the trail truly has disappeared, backtrack a few meters to see if you can regain it.
- Are there any ducks, cairns, or blazes in the area to help you re-find the trail?
- Watch for cut logs that signify past trail clearing. You can often follow an entire trail, if the area hasn't been logged for many years, by looking for cut logs.

Some types of ground just don't show trails: slickrock, granite domes, talus slopes, and scree. Look for where the trail resumes on the other side of the hard-surface terrain. Look for cairns. You can usually spot the next cairn when you are standing next to one, so look carefully.

The modern wilderness is full of cairns constructed by previous parties. These cairns are often great route-finding aids, but you should not make more. Moreover, be aware that the person who constructed those little piles might be a whole lot less experienced than you are. Use cairns in concert with your other navigational skills.

Latitude, Longitude, UTM, and MGRS

Global positioning system (GPS) devices translate signals from satellites into coordinates that you can use to plot your location on a map. Does GPS sound like the answer to your map-reading problems? Well, a GPS device is just a support tool, like a compass, and even as handheld GPS devices become less expensive, more accurate, and lighter, every navigator must still know how to read a map and relate map information to the real world. No GPS device can substitute for that ability. GPS allows us to identify and mark a discreet location on a topographic map, and there are three common methods for plotting location on a map: longitude and latitude, the UTM grid, and the MGRS grid.

LONGITUDE AND LATITUDE

Once humankind discovered that the world was a sphere, geographers developed the system of longitude and latitude to fix any location on the earth's surface.

Latitude uses a set of imaginary rings parallel to the earth's equator to measure distance north or south of the equator. These lines are called **parallels**.

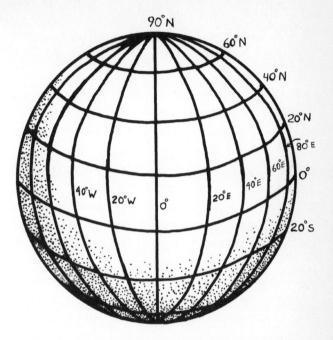

Longitude and latitude

Longitude refers to the set of imaginary rings that pass through the poles and intersect the equator at right angles. Lines of longitude are called **meridians** and they are numbered from 0 degrees to 180 degrees both east and west of the **prime meridian** (zero longitude), which passes through Greenwich, England. Lines of longitude *do not* run parallel to each other.

Latitude measures north-south distance and longitude measures east-west distance. Since the earth is a sphere, the degrees of a circle are used to number the lines of latitude and longitude.

Latitude is spoken of like this: "32 degrees north latitude" for a location in the northern hemisphere or "47 degrees south latitude" for a location in the southern hemisphere, for instance; you must specify north or south so you do not confuse locations north and south of the equator.

Longitude is referred to by the number of degrees east or west of the prime meridian: "179 degrees west longitude" for locations west of the prime meridian in Greenwich, England, and "34 degrees east longitude" for locations east of the prime meridian. You must specify east or west so you do not confuse distances east or west of the prime meridian.

The latitude and longitude of any location fixes its spot on the earth's surface. To make the system even more precise, because a degree of latitude is 111 kilometers wide, each degree of latitude and longitude is divided into 60 minutes, and each minute is divided into 60 seconds. Each second of latitude represents about 30 meters of terrain.

Latitude and Longitude Symbols

Degrees	°
Minutes	'
Seconds	"

The marks for latitude and longitude appear in the margins of topographic maps around the rectangular border of the mapped area. The degrees and minutes of the lines of latitude and longitude that enclose the mapped area (called neat-lines) are given in the margin at each of the map's corners.

In addition to the values of latitude and longitude printed at the corners, there are small slash marks, at regular intervals along the margins, that extend from the margins into the body of the map. Note that these have a value for latitude or longitude attached. Typically, this will just be the value for minutes, not the entire expression of degrees and minutes. If you want to plot positions on your map using longitude and latitude, you must connect the slash marks at the top and bottom and at each side with lines drawn in pencil along a straight edge. On a 1:24,000, 7.5-minute map the slash marks will typically be 2' 30" apart along the margins. The rectangles formed when you connect those lines encompass a lot of terrain, too much to give a precise position fix.

To locate a position to the nearest second (which *is* a precise fix) using those big squares drawn on a 7.5-minute map, use the straight edge of a piece of paper to make a minutes and seconds scale. Mark off the distance 2' 30" makes on the edge of the paper. Divide that into 15 equal lengths. Each one of those 15 lengths equals 10". So, when your GPS gives your position in degrees of latitude and longitude, find the correct 2' 30" box that includes the coordinates you have been given and use the scale you created on the straightedge to calculate the precise point indicated.

Does this system sound complicated and fraught with potential error? Well, it is. To make matters worse, near the poles it is obvious even on a large-scale map that the lines of longitude are not parallel, and you can't make a rectangle out of lines that are not parallel. It's a complicated system that makes it hard to plot an accurate location.

By the way, these problems (and indeed most map-making problems) are caused by the fact that you can't depict a curved, three-dimensional surface (the earth) on a flat, two-dimensional surface (a map) with perfect accuracy.

UNIVERSAL TRANSVERSE MERCATOR (UTM) AND MILITARY GRID REFERENCE SYSTEM (MGRS)

Fortunately, mapmakers have devised a better way to pinpoint location: a system of grid coordinates that makes it easy. The Universal Transverse Mercator (UTM) grid is the basis of the system, but the Military Grid Reference System (MGRS) refines the UTM system even further and makes it easier to use.

First, a word about the UTM grid: It does not line up perfectly with true north. Can you believe it?! One of the compromises that mapmakers have to make to project the lines of the UTM grid onto a map is that the grid doesn't orient on true north. The UTM grid orients on an imaginary place called **grid north.** Grid north is what the third north arrow points to in the map's declination diagram. So this is what the three norths are: Magnetic north, true north (at the geographic North Pole), and some imaginary reference point called grid north.

The good news about grid north is that if you're using a map with the lines of the UTM grid superimposed, you can forget about true north. With the UTM grid you convert directions between map and magnetic based on the **grid-to-magnetic angle.** This G-M angle measures the declination between grid and magnetic north. You convert directions back and forth between grid and magnetic in exactly the same manner that you do between true north and magnetic north.

It's actually much easier to measure direction on maps with the UTM grid superimposed, as the map is covered with lines oriented on grid north. Those lines make it easy to line up a compass or protractor. (Magnetic north is still magnetic north, by the way.)

How the UTM Grid Works and How to Use It to Plot Location: Grid Zone Designation

The UTM grid breaks the earth's surface into 60 grid zones from left to right, each 60 degrees wide. The grid zones are numbered from 1 to 60 and cover the entire surface of the earth except for the Arctic and Antarctic regions (between 84° and 90° N and 80° and 90° S). The two polar regions are mapped using a system called the Universal Polar Sterographic Grid, but we're going to ignore that. If you need to navigate there make sure to learn how to do it before you go.

Within each 6-degree-wide grid zone the **central meridian**—the north-south line in the exact middle of the zone—is labeled "500 000 m E" (read: GR "500,000 meters east.") The **equator**—the east-west line that divides each zone in half—serves as the 00 000 000 m N (read: "0 meters north") line for the Northern Hemisphere and as the 10 000 000 m N line for the Southern Hemisphere. (This creates south to north numbering within each hemisphere of the zone.) The whole system is metric and distances are measured in meters, which is very convenient.

Grid coordinates increase along the E-W axis as you go from left to right and along the N-S axis from bottom to top. Therefore, start at the bottom left and read grid coordinates *Right and Up,* a convention that is maintained throughout the UTM and MGRS grid systems.

Coordinate easting values count down as you run your finger left from each grid zone's 500 000 m E central meridian, and count up as you run your finger right from the central meridian. Northing values count up the number of meters north from the equator in the Northern Hemisphere and the number of meters north from the bottom of the mapped region in the Southern Hemisphere. (That's why there are two values for the equator.)

Remember, *Right and Up.*

For example, let's say that your GPS tells you that you are in grid zone 15 at 4 53 000 m E and 34 77 000 m N. You are 47 km west of the central meridian of grid zone 15 (because 500,000 m east is the central meridian and 500,000 m minus 453,000 m = 47,000 m and 47,000 m = 47 km) and 3,477,000 m N of the equator (3,477 km north of the equator).

Those coordinates locate you inside a 100,000-meter square, and, once you know what 100,000 meter square you are inside you can, for simplicity's sake, ignore the numbers to the left of the two big numbers (unless you are rapidly covering huge amounts of terrain). This would leave you with 53 000 m E and 77 000 m N.

Each 100,000-meter square is divided into 1,000-meter squares, and each 1,000-meter line has a two-digit number assigned (00–99). If you're lucky, your map will have the lines of the 1,000-meter squares superimposed. If not, you'll have to use a straightedge to pencil in the UTM grid lines by connecting the hatch marks that protrude into the map's margins.

Again, the numbers are read *Right and Up.* Run your finger along the bottom margin of the map until you hit the 53 grid line, then run your finger up the 53 grid line until you intersect the 77 grid line. You are located in the 1,000-meter square above and to the right of the intersection. This system locates a point on the earth's surface to within 1,000 meters—good, but not good enough.

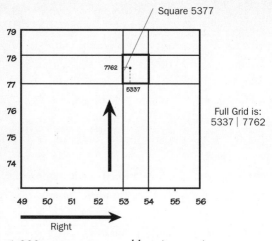

*1,000-meter squares and locating a point
to the nearest 10 meters*

The GPS lets you be much more accurate. Since the 1,000-meter squares of the UTM grid are small on a map, you can either measure in the remaining digits for 100s or even 10s of meters with a protractor, or you can just eyeball them.

53 300 m E and 77 600 m N locates the same point above to the nearest 100 meters. Again, *Right and Up,* so 53,300 is 300 meters *right* of the 53 grid line, and 77,600 is 600 meters *above* the 77 grid line.

53 370 m E and 77 620 m N locates the point above to the nearest 10 meters. Again, *Right and Up,* so 53,370 is 370 meters *right* of the 53 grid line, and 77,620 is 620 meters *above* the 77 grid line. And there shouldn't be much need to be more specific than that!

Military Grid Reference System (MGRS)

The MGRS uses a kind of shorthand to locate the correct point quickly and easily. The system works beautifully once you get used to it, and military-style maps always have the 1000-meter squares of the grid superimposed to make it easy to plot location. Note in the following example how similar the MGRS is to the UTM system. It's just the method of locating 100,000-meter squares and the written format of the coordinate that is different.

Remember the 60 zones that divide the surface of the earth in 6 degree slices? The MGRS divides each zone 20 times from bottom to top and assigns each division a letter (with "I" and "O" omitted and "A", "B", "Y", and "Z" used for the four polar zones).

The grid zone designators are read *Right and Up,* just like the UTM grid; the grid zone called out in the following illustration is read "15S."

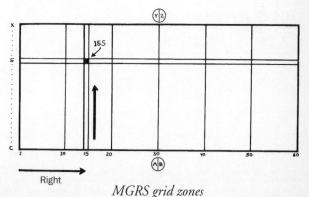

MGRS grid zones

Each grid zone is further broken into 100,000-meter squares, and each 100,000-meter square is identified with two letters—the first letter indicates what column the 100,000-meter square is in, and the second letter denotes the row. This is the same *Right and Up* system used above. For example "15SWJ."

TP	UP	VP	WP	XP	YP	
TN	UN	VN	WN	XN	YN	
TM	UM	VM	WM	XM	YM	
TL	UL	VL	WL	XL	YL	
TK	UK	VK	WK	XK	YK	**16S**
TJ	UJ	VJ	WJ	XJ	YJ	
TH	UH	VH	WH	XH	YH	
TG	UG	VG	WG	XG	YG	
TF	UF	VF	WF	XF	YF	

100,000-meter squares

So "15SWJ5377" refers to the 1,000-meter square in grid zone 15S, in 100,000-meter square "WJ" (in grid zone 15S), and 1,000-meter grid line 53 read *Right* and 1,000-meter grid line 77 read *Up*. This system locates a specific point on the earth's surface to within 1,000 meters. For simplicity's sake, the "15S" part of the coordinate is almost always dropped and the "WJ" part is usually dropped, except when you're near a boundary or using small-scale maps where confusion could erupt.

To locate the same point to the nearest 100 meters, we make a further division in the coordinate system. Again, this is done *Right and Up,* so 533776 (dropping the "15SWJ") might locate the point above to the nearest 100 meters. Note how the grid has expanded from 4 to 6 digits, so we split the coordinate in half, and the first half is the right coordinate and the second part is the up coordinate. 533 is 300 meters *right* of the 53 grid line, and 776 is 600 meters *above* the 77 grid line.

The same thing happens when we get even more specific and locate a point to the nearest 10 meters. 53377762 means that the location is 370 meters right of the 53 grid line and 620 meters above the 77 grid line.

So the full MGRS coordinate for the point in our example is 15SWJ53377762. The MGRS grid takes a little getting used to, but it is the best system for location. Let's hope that someday soon we see the grid superimposed on every topo map.

Where Are You Right Now?

The human tradition of navigation is an old one; it is thrilling to travel in the same vein as Columbus, Magellan, and Lewis and Clark. Their basic navigational problem was the same as yours: Where am I *Right Now*?

The techniques of map analysis, terrain association, and dead reckoning are the fundamental skills of land navigation. They are very powerful tools with which you will be able to analyze maps, relate the real world to the map world, and locate where you are *Right Now*.

Wilderness route finding is a metaphor for life. A traveler in the wilderness charts his or her progress by pinpointing, repeatedly, his or her position *Right Now*. The traveler's destination provides direction. Success is cemented by the painstaking grind of here and now.

Unfortunately, the life-navigation metaphor does not automatically work in reverse. Just because you know where you are *Right Now* when navigating in the wilderness does not mean that you know where you are right now on the path of life. But perhaps it helps.